ALSO BY RICHIE HOFMANN

*Second Empire*
*A Hundred Lovers*

# THE BRONZE ARMS

# THE BRONZE ARMS

· POEMS ·

Richie Hofmann

ALFRED A. KNOPF
NEW YORK
2026

A BORZOI BOOK
FIRST HARDCOVER EDITION
PUBLISHED BY ALFRED A. KNOPF 2026



Published by Alfred A. Knopf, a division of Penguin Random House LLC,
1745 Broadway, New York, NY 10019.

Knopf, Borzoi Books, and the colophon are registered trademarks of
Penguin Random House LLC.

LIBRARY OF CONGRESS CATALOGING-IN-PUBLICATION DATA
Names: Hofmann, Richie, 1987– author
http://id.loc.gov/authorities/names/n2015011091
http://id.loc.gov/rwo/agents/n2015011091
Title: The bronze arms : poems / Richie Hofmann.
Other titles: Bronze arms (Compilation)
http://id.loc.gov/resources/hubs/7fd7ee27-88d2-b644-b69e-e3cee124ec5f
Identifiers: LCCN 2025010080 (print) | LCCN 2025010081 (ebook) |
ISBN 9780593804742 hardcover | ISBN 9780593804759 ebook
Subjects: LCGFT: Poetry
http://id.loc.gov/authorities/genreForms/gf2014026481
Classification: LCC PS3608.O4798 B76 2026 (print) |
LCC PS3608.O4798 (ebook) | DDC 811/.6—dc23/eng/20250610
LC record available at https://lccn.loc.gov/2025010080
LC ebook record available at https://lccn.loc.gov/2025010081

penguinrandomhouse.com | aaknopf.com

Printed in Canada
2 4 6 8 9 7 5 3 1

The authorized representative in the EU for product safety and compliance is Penguin Random House Ireland, Morrison Chambers, 32 Nassau Street, Dublin D02 YH68, Ireland, https://eu-contact.penguin.ie.

# CONTENTS

# THE BRONZE ARMS

# The Bronze Arms

Love is a memory now, you said.
Most of the bronzes have been melted down
and made into other bronzes,
coins, weapons—

Love is a memory now,
you said to me.
If antiquity can survive, love can too.

But it must be forceful.

# Minotaur

There was sand in my camera lens.

It ruined the edges of every picture I have of you.

I stood at the end of the room.

A villa and then there were the clouds.

I drink: The sea is there.

It was hot: I wore shorts with a drawstring.

Eating ice cream. Chasing pigeons.

Listening for the mooing of the tourists.

The meals we ate had a wounded beauty.

The city a construction site.

My longing for you followed me like a shadow,

Getting longer in the day, disappearing at night, the maze

Where they sacrificed boys.

A maze of light and shadows.

In myths, the gods are slaves to passion.

They don't die

Of hunger. Night

On the beach: I watch you walk into the water.

Pay attention to me.

There's music a couple streets over: It's the Eurythmics.

You could have drowned me

And no one would have known.

I can't stop looking at you,

At the black of your groin.

And the small towel we share:

Teal with stripes.

# Breed Me

My sweat soaked the sheets.

You used to be like everyone else

But then

The way you hurt me (fingers, teeth):

I grew accustomed to it

Then I craved it

Then I got bored

And other men tried to put death into my mouth.

Angelic Richie with bite marks

In such a clean room.

I deplore clutter but I do like flowers.

A tall drinking glass filled with peonies

The color of underwear.

I like hard and classical.

The ceiling black like Caravaggio's wine.

Through the blinds, obscure gods shined,

Making the outlines of my body

A kind of emptiness.

The ceiling fan

Pushed heat around

Even though it was snowing outside.

You forgave

My love of surfaces.

It's not a tragedy we couldn't have a child.

I had a pain inside me

And I needed you to deepen it.

he chewed my hair softly
while I slept on his chest
any fragment of him unhinges me
masters me

in that short time when I'm not conscious
all the heads are replaced
names are scratched off the coins
no one remembers me

to wake me once
he shoved crumpled dollar bills in my mouth
over black coffee I told him my favorite emperor castrated a slave
and made him his wife

I'm so tired of beauty
when I sleep in my underwear
black flies land on my shoulders
clean as the afterlife

# Lust Archive

A night in the claw-foot tub.

The water covers my face.

I taste it and remember.

The tap water

In Rome, in Vilnius, in Kep—

Putting my mouth under the spigot,

Sucking it down hard.

Serenity and violence,

Pleasure and loneliness,

In Venice.

The six Titians

In one place in Boston,

United for the first time since Philip II used them

To get hard for his ugly wife

With whom he had to have a child.

Danaë's soft body, Venus's bare feet—

Women from the front and behind—

Diana washing her armpits,

Callisto swollen

With Jupiter's baby,

Andromeda chained at her wrists and ankles,

The only other man

Ripped apart by hounds,

Europa gripping the bull's

One horn as he kidnaps her—

In twenty-four hours,

We were in an apartment,

A hotel with blackout shades,

And your parents' house.

Mouth of a god, mouth of a lover:

I was writhing, sucking.

And then I was alone,

The hunger

Not yet drained from me

Like the tap water.

I didn't drown, it wasn't a rape, you let me go.

A couple drops

Still dripped

Like a portrait's diamonds.

morning we ruin the surface
with two opaline cords of piss

the weirdest urge     write your name
in your manly handwriting
right on my skin
in permanent marker

the night entering the day from behind
I took off my clothes
my body a series of entrances and exits
desire     desire without any meaning

# Young People

He was stirring coffee in his workout clothes.

I wanted to swallow him,

Coffee black in my stomach.

The sun was moving in the glass of buildings.

He was sweating, he was late,

I was suffering from beauty,

Thirstiest in the morning,

Sleeping in my T-shirt with stiff yellow armpits.

His belly was so warm.

He knew my name.

I could taste almonds in his mouth.

Tell me I own you, Richie.

Don't forget it.

The hours we didn't do anything

But sit on the floor in silence:

Nothing more erotic than being in the same room

Not interacting—

Reading different articles,

Our minds elsewhere,

The sky becoming white then black,

That submissive sleep

On the bed I gave to

My friend's sister when I moved.

# Armour / Amour

It should end with us meeting on the bus,

The camera around your neck,

My tote bag stuffed with paperbacks,

My beloved dead saying:

Be restrained.

Try to sneak

A blurry photograph before you get off

And see something disgraceful.

You could lick the fear off my skin.

You could lick the sunscreen off my legs.

Your flesh and photographs,

My desire to be captive.

Put your camera in my mouth.

My heart throws itself

Against my ribs. If you capture

Other men

Here with us, they are ghosts—

But nothing ethereal

About them, they reek.

That blurry photograph makes me think of the underworld,

Of all the strangers

Not coming back, developing

Into abstractions.

My beloved dead saying:

Be restrained.

the end of love isn't like a death
I would come back
your hand over my mouth
don't ever take it off

if I sleep alone
all your dead lovers sleep inside me

my flesh kisses the glove of leather
the chain
the bed
the tether

I can't help lying there like a slain boy
if you bleed in the dust
if the blood turns to beauty
if the beauty turns to nothing

# Armed Cavalier

The end of autumn

Lowers its leaves

In the wealthy residential neighborhoods.

Paintings in galleries and private foundations

Hold some short-lived way of seeing

Into misery or love.

Those artists believed in power.

I should, too.

Strangers unman me

In a rented studio. And each time, something

Empties out of me,

Disquieting, delicate. My heart

Is sulphur, my body

Pasty in daylight, the dead my only

Readers now.

The bathroom: The tub, sink, and toilet are empty.

We should lock ourselves in here for a whole weekend

And not eat or drink.

I'm not actually a trapped animal, I could leave,

I don't want to.

Let's play that game where I'm the dead bird from *The Hours*.

A quail chick a hunter puts to sleep

To train the dogs.

The liver is the seat of lust.

You should cut it out of me and eat it.

I want poems to be memories

Of my ancestors, calling them back.

The end of autumn

Unfolds in a series of textures and places:

Rough towels, the laundry,

The green walls of a place I belonged to.

Stars, slow traffic,

The summer I wished you loved me

Enough to kill me,

But not really.

The airport outside Berlin,

The arms of others.

My childhood is over, I only sleep in this bed now.

# Maze

Room of flowers,
room of hunger: the hours
I could sleep inside.

There was something I wanted
my life to be. Room
in which I possessed someone

and was in turn possessed.
Rooms in which I reached for a man,
even when he

was with someone else.
Once I was so scared,
I slept in my shoes.

Another time, I stood knee-deep
in chlorinated water
and thought I'd be lost

forever: the graffiti
unintelligible, the smell
of cigarettes, the foreign tongues.

Still, the jets of the whirlpool pulsated.
I dried off; I made
the damp towel a pillow.

The crowded rooms
of the bars made them cool.
Young people were shouting

                                        into my ears.
                              I was growing up,
like them and not

                              like them.
                    In the tall mirror,
I could see my back.

                              Was this
how I was going to live?
                              I took long baths

                    in quiet rooms. Room of jealousy,
room of flowers—sometimes
          I felt pulled forward

                                        as if a perfect leash
were guiding me. Other times
                    from behind, knuckles nudging

the small of my back,
                              urging me deeper
          in pajama bottoms

toward other rooms.

# Maze

The pool-water clings
to his skin.
A techno remix coming in

and out. My mouth fills
with water. I think
of my swimming lessons

in Munich
in another century.
Frau Instructor,

her gruesome armpit.
She points wildly
into the lap lane, yells to go faster.

The smell of chlorine
is the smell of hatred
of the body.

German isn't scary.
Any language
shouted at you militaristically

sounds a little ugly.
He is rough
in the apartment

and tender outside.
No towel for you.
Dry yourself.

It’s crazy—
you can know
and forget

a whole language.
And here we are,
saying what we feel.

We weren’t sentenced
to death
by the government,

priests, or our fathers,
but centuries of hatred
have made us lovers.

# Lamb

I had a lamb I brought everywhere

Who only had one eye.

At the train stations,

All the grown-ups would say, be mindful

Of your things, little boy,

Someone will steal right out of your pocket

Or take the watch off your wrist.

My dad had a beautiful overcoat.

The lamb's white fur got smudged.

My brother was a baby,

And in the restaurants,

The old waiters would pick him up

And kiss him again and again on the cheek

With their mustaches

And tell my parents

That they promised they would bring him back in a minute

But now they needed to show the chef.

I don't remember when the eye became unglued

And who knows where it went.

On long train rides,

I remember falling asleep,

Putting my finger in the hole where it used to be.

Once he had to go in an overhead bin,

And he was freezing when I kissed him again.

# Drowning on Crete

Before I died,

I was pulled out of the water.

It only took half a minute.

I wasn't wearing anything.

I was five.

Bottles of soda must have fallen from the chaise.

But I heard nothing.

I was below the water

And earth, where boys die,

Not knowing where to go.

Nothing to do in the hidden rooms

But lie down and wait.

Light was coming through a ceiling.

What would rescue even look like?

Painted on the vase,

Dark orange on black,

My parents hold my small body.

Their tears are wet like my hair.

I swallow water.

The sun is strong,

The sea smells like men's bodies.

I didn't die

But for one moment

I was someone who would never be old.

# Arms

Even far from home, we felt safe.

We walked around the ruins. Bodies of men whose heads and privates

Were smashed off. None of the statues had arms.

We heard about the boy

Who drowned while swimming

With a dolphin.

Later we were by the pool.

My father read

A magazine. I could see pictures in his sunglasses

When he turned a page.

On the island where boys drown,

I remember his arms pulling me from the water,

An archaeologist in a bathing suit.

The night was humid, the stone he put me down on

Warm. It would have been a catastrophe for my father,

But it wouldn't have changed a thing in the world.

I was a boy who drowned, the old women would say,

Drawn from the water

By his father's arms.

The tide came in.

You wouldn't have known there was ever a beach.

marble dust blown by the breeze
flecks of the ideal body
have I ever inhaled it

ugly America sleeps
and boys my age run with sweat in their hair
the momentary flash
of their skin in the sea

the stars swallow each other
the waves are absorbed
so much pain rushes through
my love of beautiful things

the night loves my young body
a boy held captive by a friend's wrists
I won't ever forget the polished white
of the urinals

what I feel is excruciating hunger
what's the point of kissing
one day I'll lick men's arms

time will waste us
the deep sea swallows everything
will make us feminine
and bend us

# Dolphin

*(HERMIAS OF IASOS)*

A dolphin fell in love with me.
Probably because of my looks—
people always said, What a pretty boy you are.

I was coming home from Gymnasium,
I was so sweaty from running,
we all were, we all ran into the sea,
its freshness,
we gargled the water, we threw it from our hair—

I washed my limbs in the waves,
and I heard him calling.

I didn't want the other boys to see.

But I kept glancing at the shimmering sea,
hoping he was there. My dolphin.
I dreamed about becoming
a dolphin, being carried
on the waves, doing flips while the boys clapped from the docks,
chasing the elegant boats,
making choreography in their wakes.
I dreamed.

The sight of a dolphin is always
a little bit magical,
even on our island.

But he liked that I was human.
That is why he fell in love with me.
Because I wasn't a dolphin.
He liked my singing voice.
I blushed, but I knew he thought I was good
at singing made-up songs.

I never liked animals,
not really trusting something
that doesn't talk.
But I knew what he felt.

One day I walked right into the water.
I was surprised by how his skin felt.
Pricklier than it looks.
He let me put my mouth to his blowhole
Oh my god
it was the saltiest thing I tasted.
I held on to his fin and we swam, he always dove up
so I could breathe.

I came home exhilarated.
My parents were mad I dripped all over the house,
dragging my wet feet across the floor,
dripping onto the pillows
and the white blankets.

Why are you swimming all evening?
When there's homework to be done!
My mother said she could smell the salt
and it disgusted her.
Take a shower right now.

Night entered the sea.
Night where there is no future.

I imagined his gray body against the waves.
I sat in our courtyard with olive trees.
Gulls laughed at me,
the open door.

Waking from the incomplete dream,
I wanted to possess him—
What a weird thing for a child to say, I know.

Dolphins carried Dionysus to the underworld,
disappearing each winter—
Would mine carry me there?
Winter came.
The constellations
disappeared.

It's terrible what happens next, but our playing
turned rough. It was an accident.
I was bleeding
in the water, I hardly noticed at first,

but then the panic set in.
I started thrashing in the water.
My dolphin wanted to save me.

He hadn't meant to cut my flesh
with his sharp fin,
the salt was stinging.

I died onshore, my dolphin tossed me there.
And he flung himself there, too,
to die beside me.

I am a little famous.
I was loved by a dolphin.

They minted coins that showed us playing.
I never thought
they would miss me.

And they make songs about us,
the humans,
saying that dolphins were human once,
and charmed by singing.

# Allegory of Love

Love jerked me up by my hair and told me I was its slave.
It was 6 a.m., I didn't even know.
Ouch, I said.
It pressed down on me.

I searched around to give it something.
My expensive shirt was on the floor.
But my mortal body was the only currency.
So we made love

the way other men subordinate beasts or submit
to tyranny.
It held on to my wrists.
It didn't let me shave.

I'm going to have you forever,
it told me.
You can have me for a while,
I said.

# Pantheon

The city was getting wet.

Pigeons hovered like unclean angels.

I ruined my leather slippers

In the streets. Construction shook us,

Dust covered all surfaces

Of the apartment. How far should you dig

To go to the heart of the past:

The city piled on the graves, the century

Passing over all of it—

The Neoclassical, the Brutalist, each with their ideas

Of how to live.

The radio played politics.

Big tough men in the squares, some on horseback,

Pointed backward with delicate fingers.

I played death-games

With my friend's belt with the Tiffany buckle

Until his initials were on my neck.

I listened to Lieder, and I felt the human soul

Talking to me.

There were so many other men

Who mixed their pleasures

Then disappeared.

What if nothing were hidden between us?

What if freedom could lift us out of the dark pool

Like my dad once did

When I didn't die

And was young?

what was I looking for
I knew I wouldn't find it
rain punishing the cemeteries and the train stations
sea hurting the beach of stones

the gods don't die
we do
I don't love them
I don't love them enough to give them my death

# Maze

Horny, half-mad,
the smell of old flowers
encases

this man's room
like an anonymous
tomb—miracle

to be alive
and then to die. In the thick
of an island thick

with a history
that belongs to
everyone and no one,

feral goats shit and mate
and clamber in dust,
kicking it up.

Don't you hate animals?
Don't you hate
being an animal?

His animal? This
animal? Still it feels good
when the sun comes up

and warms the bed
like the cold surface
of the ancient ocean.

And by midday, no shade
anywhere.
When did the flowers first die?

When did they stop drinking
water from the vase?
Water-colored linen

when nights
are spent naked
and animal-like

in his arms,
entrapped by sleep,
human sleep, sleep

which separates
me from lover
and also from self. So obedient.

# Maze

The streetlamps made the leaves
black. The night
is a place of initiation.

Virgins get fed to it.
Beaches and ruins.
Skeletal buildings.

The trees were young
but the marble was old.
My jaw hurt.

I was young
but my dream was old.
A force

was galloping toward me.
I took a bus, a bus
with locked windows

to get here.
The thing I looked for—
I knew him by his beard.

My skin touched
his mouth—
saliva, cooked meat, red wine.

Back home, the kids were cruel to me.
When I was happy
they called me

a faggot
to puncture that happiness.
I was holding a rope,

walking down to the unlit beach.
I could hear grown men yelping.
I hid my glasses

in a bathing suit pocket.
The thing I was looking for—
he was an animal

who followed me. The lover
a faceless
presence. But I

saw his face.
His watch-face glowed.
When he saw I was bleeding

in my ugly sandals,
he said, You can go home,
I won't hurt you.

# Black-Figure

A room of fragile things:

We looked at paintings on vases:

We watched something secret,

And the pain was breaking inside me.

Any stranger's eyes were hooks.

The guards at the museums,

Younger than we are,

With black machine guns

Across their narrow chests.

My feet black from walking around the city in flip-flops.

A black that has every color in it.

My feet made your sheets dirty,

Your pillows that smelled like chemical chamomile.

We didn't spend anything between us,

No black aftertaste of love, no fear,

As the hard smooth light

Drowned the room, and I fell asleep

And the hours turned, and I woke up,

And the black band of your trackpants

Made a line on my skin.

Just yesterday, I was sitting on the asphalt,

Then driving in the back of a black car—dozing,

Voraciously alone.

# Men's Beds

I was promiscuous

With my feelings most of all.

Under stars,

I sprayed saline solution into two wineglasses

And took out my contacts.

I didn't want summer to end, but it did.

Many lives

Happened inside those walls,

And for a season,

I wore a designer hoodie

And got iced americanos every morning.

I slept in men's beds:

They took turns breaking

Me. It felt good, but one's absence

Weighed on me like a death.

Late summer blurred

Feelings together

With rain.

At least I wasn't going to be lonely.

I moved around the city,

Buying paperbacks,

Putting sunscreen on my neck.

Who hasn't yearned for a stranger?

The trains were free.

I mean: No one checked your ticket.

Eros grabs me
Eros tells me what to do
you're going to live   says Eros
you're going to live inside your flesh

# The Bronzes

Arms reach up from the sand.
An amateur scuba diver finds them.

*

He thinks it is a dead body at first.
But the arms are bronze.

*

Soon they are lifted from the water.
Bodies sprung fully formed—

*

their calcite eyes and silver teeth,
their lips and nipples copper.

*

There are two of them, both with beards.
Like a father and son.

*

Even though they're soldiers, their poses are so relaxed.
Their faces kind and gentle like people on vacation.

*

No wreck or anything survives.
Maybe they were being stolen.

*

This year it's been fifty years above the water again.
That was before I was born.

*

Everything seemed to happen back then.
Like being asleep, then being awake.

*

Men can tell you time isn't real
but look at all it's done.

*

Masculine arms lifted me.
Masculine arms held me while I slept.

*

I woke up stinking,
breaking the surface of my life.

*

Something was lost, something wrecked.
Something looted, something recovered.

*

My back to your chest,
my feet perched on yours.

*

We would know one another's body
in any context now.

*

I could be bronze,
my blue eyes flecked with gold,

*

I could belong to you
or belong to no one.

the statues are broken
they still have their young bodies

it's so sweet to be asleep
dreaming of dark drills
quarrying marble

heads of boys with cold white hair
looted things

# Night Star

Footfall in the long hallways above us,

Painted stars on the ceiling, real stars from the balcony.

Teenagers were making out

By the public fountain.

You had a terrible apartment: The sinkwater tasted like blood.

I cut my fingernails over the toilet.

My parents were still married in another country.

Young swallows were dropping themselves.

For a whole weekend,

I wore one of your shirts.

That will mean the most to me

In my short life. There was a big wormwood armoire

With an urn on top.

You said those were the landlady's ashes.

The mattress made a sound as you lay down.

My shoulders were sunburned,

It hurt when you pulled my arm out of one sleeve,

I tasted your deodorant as the shirt came off.

Fall came and disappeared.

We were meant to live another life.

I mean here.

you won't remember me
kissed your mouth
kissed the cross around your neck
left the room in my socks so you wouldn't hear

specters hang over the city in the most quotidian ways
winter like milk
you should have crushed me

crush me delicately

the year was a room
a noiseless maze to lose myself in
pungent   stupid dream
I want to remember everything that didn't happen

# Night Autobiography

A love so penetrating

It is always unreturned:

That's been the organizing desire

Of my life.

There are ghosts in these streets, in these faucets,

In the radiators

That hiss all night and make me so hot

I wake up covered in sweat.

It's no wonder I've wasted months at a time.

Nights spent

Playing ostentatious music.

For many nights,

I was the misfit, the broken one, the one

No one ever would love.

But then one night

A bearded man slid his fingers in my underwear

And said to his friend, So clean.

I like how pink your body is.

Do you want it gentle? one night asked.

I want it hard, said another night.

Saint Hervé, I will honor your earthly

Ambition. I will write dead letters

To you and all the others sent away

To the underworld.

In my short life, I've fallen in love, but that's mostly it.

Taken in the dark

And humiliated

By the deep sea.

## Elegant Perversion

It was freezing in the unheated churches.

My hair was uncombed,

My eyes couldn't close.

Eyes of the ruling class dead

Stared down.

Underneath an expensive coat,

I had hairy legs and a classical phallus.

I wanted to be blindfolded.

The hallways of a villa

Filled with ghosts of illegitimate children—

Those were the voices

I heard in your apartment,

Scratching the headboard.

Rain in the ashtray, rain in the broken chair.

In the books stacked around us,

People bled over lust

For women. In public toilets,

Piss tethered strangers

To the wall, their hair flattened

By rain. When it rained,

The squares flooded like the urinals.

You like it here, or you don't.

It's climate change and unbridled tourism.

Also the punishment

Of the grim gods of water.

Their faces line the facades, each one

With a different feeling:

I am hungry, I am powerful,

I am lustful, I am defeated.

I lay awake feigning sleep, everything bronze.

The water opaque like coffee

Swallows the buildings,

I play dead in your arms.

# ACKNOWLEDGMENTS

Endless gratitude to Deborah Garrison and to the editors of the following magazines:

Academy of American Poets Poem-a-Day: "Lamb"
*The Atlantic:* "Night Star"
*Classical Philology:* "Eros grabs me"
*The New Republic:* "The Bronze Arms"
*The New Yorker:* "Arms"
*The Paris Review:* "Armed Cavalier"
*Peripheries:* "Maze" (II)
*Poetry:* "Breed Me," "Dolphin," "Pantheon"
*The Sewanee Review:* "Maze" (I), "Maze" (III), "Maze" (IV)
*The Yale Review:* "Young People"

## A NOTE ABOUT THE AUTHOR

Richie Hofmann is the recipient of fellowships from the Guggenheim Foundation and the National Endowment for the Arts. His poetry appears in two previous books, *A Hundred Lovers* (2022) and *Second Empire* (2015), and in *The Paris Review, The New Yorker, Poetry, The New Republic,* and *The Yale Review.*

## A NOTE ON THE TYPE

This book was set in Adobe Garamond. Designed for the Adobe Corporation by Robert Slimbach, the fonts are based on types first cut by Claude Garamond (ca. 1480–1561). It is to Garamond that we owe the letter we now know as "old style." He gave to his letters an elegance and feeling of movement that won him an immediate reputation and the patronage of Francis I of France.

*Composed by North Market Street Graphics*
*Lancaster, Pennsylvania*

*Book design by Pei Loi Koay*